WORLD OF VOCABULARY

TAN

Sidney J. Rauch

Alfred B. Weinstein

Assisted by Muriel Harris

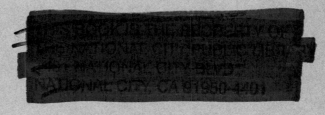

GLOBE FEARON
Pearson Learning Group

1 SALSA STAR

øRubén Blades is a man of many **talents.** He is a **composer,** a singer, an actor, and even a lawyer. Blades writes and sings *salsa* songs. (The word *salsa* means "hot sauce" in Spanish.)

Most *salsa* songs are dance tunes. But Blades's songs tell important stories we do not usually hear about in songs. Blades sings about the evils of greed and laziness. Some of his songs are about his love of truth and **justice.**

Blades's acting career has added to his fame. He played a sheriff in the movie *The Milagro Beanfield War*. He **appeared** with Jack Nicholson in *The Two Jakes*. He acted with Joe Pesci in the film *The Super*.

Rubén Blades was born in Panama in 1948. He came to the United States in 1974. Now that he is famous, Blades is trying to **aid** the poor people of Panama. He wants to improve the living conditions of his people.

Although Rubén Blades is a Harvard-educated lawyer, he has not yet used his **legal** training. But Blades is thinking of a career in government. When people ask if he would ever run for the office of president of Panama, Blades **responds,** "Why not?" For this **singular** man, anything is possible.

MAKE A LIST

>>>> *There are eight vocabulary words in this lesson. In the story, they are boxed in color. Copy the vocabulary words here.*

1. _____   5. _____

2. _____   6. _____

3. _____   7. _____

4. _____   8. _____

MAKE AN ALPHABETICAL LIST

>>>> Here are the eight words you copied on the previous page. Write them in alphabetical order in the spaces below.

justice	legal	composer	responds
talents	aid	singular	appeared

1. _____   5. _____

2. _____   6. _____

3. _____   7. _____

4. _____   8. _____

WHAT DO THE WORDS MEAN?

>>>> *Following are some meanings, or definitions, for the eight vocabulary words in this lesson. Write the words next to their definitions.*

1. _____ answers; replies

2. _____ was seen (on stage or screen); performed

3. _____ a person who writes music

4. _____ having to do with the law or with lawyers

5. _____ to help; to give what is useful or necessary

6. _____ fairness; rightfulness

7. _____ worthy of notice; remarkable

8. _____ special or natural abilities; skills

>>>> It is important to know the short vowel sounds. Remember: the vowels are *a, e, i, o, u,* and sometimes *y.*

Below are some words that contain the short vowel sounds. Look at them carefully and say them slowly. Stretch out the sounds so you can hear the vowels.

You will notice that when there is just one vowel sound in a word, it has the short vowel sound. A short vowel is marked by putting a small curved mark—for example, *ŭ*—above the letter.

>>>> Here are two samples of each of the short vowels.

short ă	short ĕ	short ĭ	short ŏ	short ŭ
măt	lĕt	fĭt	ŏx	ŭp
băttle	bĕd	fĭddle	bŏttle	ŭnder

>>>> *Underline each word in parentheses that has a short vowel sound. Then draw a ˘ above the short vowel.*

1. Susan left the (plate, <u>dĭsh</u>) on the table.

2. If you (shake, rock) the tree, the apples will fall.

3. We have a large (pile, stack) of coins.

4. I don't know why he (yells, screams) so much.

5. (Jane, Jan) was the first one in line for tickets.

6. Our puppy plays (cute, funny) tricks.

>>>> A **synonym** is a word that means the same, or nearly the same, as another word. *Happy* and *glad* are synonyms.

>>>> *The column on the left contains the eight key words in the story. To the right of each key word are three other words or groups of words. Two of these are synonyms for the key word. Circle the two synonyms.*

1.	**aid**	to assist	to harm	to help
2.	**justice**	rightfulness	fair play	conduct
3.	**talents**	abilities	celebrations	skills
4.	**singular**	extraordinary	unnoticed	amazing
5.	**appeared**	performed	came into view	vanished
6.	**responds**	asks	says	replies
7.	**composer**	creator	song writer	singer
8.	**legal**	having to do with the law	having to do with eagles	having to do with lawyers

>>>> *In each of the following sentences, there are words that need capital letters. Rewrite each sentence with the words correctly capitalized. Remember that capital letters are used in the following places: in the first word in a sentence; names of people, cars, cities, states, countries; days of the week; months of the year.*

1. when rubén blades came to the united states from panama, he was 26 years old.

   _____

   _____

2. rubén blades sang at the salsa festival, which was held at madison square garden in new york city.

   _____

   _____

3. he won his first grammy award for the album "escenas," which included a song with linda ronstadt.

   _____

   _____

USE YOUR OWN WORDS

>>>> *Look at the picture. What words come into your mind other than the ones you just matched with their synonyms? Write them on the lines below. To help you get started, here are two good words:*

1. _____ smile _____
2. _____ mustache _____
3. _____
4. _____

5. _____
6. _____
7. _____
8. _____

COMPLETE THE STORY

>>>> Here are the eight vocabulary words for this lesson:

singular	appeared	aid	justice
composer	talents	legal	responds

>>>> *There are four blank spaces in the story below. Four vocabulary words have already been used in the story. They are underlined. Use the other four words to fill in the blanks.*

Rubén Blades is a <u>composer</u> who was born in Panama. He sings his own salsa songs. These are not dance tunes. Blades has _____ on stage to sing about the kind of world he would like to live in. In this world, all people would be treated fairly.

Blades has other _____. He is also an actor. Some of his movies include *The Milagro Beanfield War*, *The Two Jakes*, and *The Super*.

Blades is a lawyer, too. Sometimes people ask him <u>legal</u> questions. They know Blades can <u>aid</u> them with his advice. People listen carefully when he _____.

Years of hard work have made Blades famous. But he hasn't forgotten the people of Panama. He cares about their needs for <u>justice</u> and better living conditions. His songs have given them hope. Now he wants to do more. Rubén Blades is truly a _____ person.

Learn More About Panama

>>>> *On a separate piece of paper or in your notebook or journal, complete one or more of the activities below.*

Learning Across the Curriculum

The Panama Canal, completed in 1914, changed the way ships traveled around the Americas. Research how the canal was created and draw a map that explains where the canal is.

Broadening Your Understanding

Imagine that Rubén Blades is running for president of Panama. Write a brief paragraph telling why you think people might or might not vote for him.

2 REBEL IN RHYTHM

The spotlight is on Twyla Tharp and the dancers. The dancers whirl like tops and tumble in **rotation.** While dancing, they look like the blinking colors in a neon sign. They move with the speed of light. The audience cheers. **Bouquets** of flowers are tossed on stage in honor of a great performance.

Twyla Tharp, the **rebel** of dance, has made it. She is one of America's **major** choreographers (kohree AHG raf erzs). Her job is to arrange the dances and direct the dancers. Tharp **combines** jazz and classical music in her work. Most of her dances are done on a plain stage with very little **scenery.** Sometimes she sets her dances to varied **background** music. But she doesn't always use music. Then all you hear are the dancers' breathing and the movements of their feet.

Tharp worked hard to become a world famous choreographer. As a teen, she put in long hours practicing her dance and music. She studied with many leading dancers. She believed there was a **grand** plan for her to become a star. Tharp's mother agreed that her daughter would be famous. She was so sure of this that she even changed the spelling of her daughter's name. *Twila* became *Twyla* because she thought it would look better in lights!

MAKE A LIST

>>>> *There are eight vocabulary words in this lesson. In the story, they are boxed in color. Copy the vocabulary words here.*

1. _____   5. _____

2. _____   6. _____

3. _____   7. _____

4. _____   8. _____

MAKE AN ALPHABETICAL LIST

>>>> *Here are the eight words you copied on the previous page. Write them in alphabetical order in the spaces below.*

bouquets	scenery	rebel	combines
background	rotation	grand	major

1. _____
2. _____
3. _____
4. _____

5. _____
6. _____
7. _____
8. _____

WHAT DO THE WORDS MEAN?

>>>> *Following are some meanings, or definitions, for the eight vocabulary words in this lesson. Write the words next to their definitions.*

1. _____ a person who goes against the system; one who resists authority

2. _____ large; important; complete

3. _____ bunches of flowers fastened together

4. _____ taking turns in a regular order; one following the other

5. _____ painted pictures or hangings for a stage

6. _____ joins together; mixes

7. _____ main; principal

8. _____ accompanying the main action

It is important to know the vowels in the alphabet. They are *a, e, i, o, u,* and sometimes *y.*

When a vowel in a word has the same sound as its name, it is called a **long vowel.** The long vowel is marked by putting a line above the letter, like: ā, ē, ī, ō, ū.

Here are two samples of each of the long vowels.

long ā	**long ē**	**long ī**
cāke	wē	bīke
wāde	Pēte	fīre

long ō	**long ū**	**sometimes ȳ**
drōve	mūsic	happȳ (long e sound)
grōw	hūman	crȳ (long i sound)

Look at the following words. Underline the words that have long vowel sounds and put a line above the long vowel. The first one has been done as an example.

tūbe   baby   store   pan   dime

flop   claw   made   ice   slow

Underline each word in parentheses that has a long vowel sound. Then draw a line above the long vowel.

1. Did you get that (glove, robe) for your birthday?
2. I (made, bought) a plane for my science class.
3. Lindbergh flew (swiftly, solo) across the Atlantic Ocean.
4. Would you like to be a (dancer, musician) one day?
5. Can you (ride, sit) on your horse?
6. I'll race you to the (lake, pond).

FIND THE SYNONYMS

>>>> A **synonym** is a word that means the same, or nearly the same, as another word. *Happy* and *glad* are synonyms.

>>>> *The column on the left contains the eight key words in the story. To the right of each key word are three other words or groups of words. Two of these are synonyms for the key word. Circle the two synonyms.*

1.	**bouquets**	green plants	bunches of flowers	flowers tied together
2.	**major**	principal	serious	main
3.	**rotation**	taking turns	speaking clearly	one after another
4.	**scenery**	audience	stage pictures	stage hangings
5.	**background**	future plans	in the back	accompanying part
6.	**rebel**	one who acts against authority	one who joins the crowd	one who goes against the system
7.	**combines**	separates	joins	mixes
8.	**grand**	important	small	large

14

>>>> An **adjective** is a word that describes a person, place, or thing. For example, in the sentence, "Twyla Tharp is a talented dancer," *talented* is the word that describes *dancer*.

>>>> *Underline the adjectives in the sentences below.*

1. Twyla Tharp never expected to be a famous dancer.

2. Her dancers often perform on a bare stage with simple scenery.

3. After graduation, she continued studying with some of the best dance teachers.

4. A good dancer recognizes the value of an excellent teacher.

5. By combining jazz and classical ballet, Twyla has created exciting new dances.

USE YOUR OWN WORDS

>>>> *Look at the picture. What words come into your mind other than the ones you matched with their synonyms? Write them on the lines below. To help you get started, here are two good words:*

1. performers

2. dancing

3.

4.

5.

6.

7.

8.

COMPLETE THE STORY

>>>> Here are the eight vocabulary words for this lesson:

rebel	combines	grand	rotation
background	scenery	major	bouquets

>>>> *There are four blank spaces in the story below. Four vocabulary words have already been used in the story. They are underlined. Use the other four words to fill in the blanks.*

Ballet has become an important art form in America. One of the people most responsible is Twyla Tharp. She has often been called a _____ because she does the unexpected. She combines jazz and classical ballet to form new routines. Sometimes she uses little or no scenery and no music. Her dancers perform unusual steps in rotation. They have been carefully trained by Tharp.

Tharp always believed there was a _____ plan that pointed her toward stardom. Her plan was helped by her _____ and good training in dance and music. She studied musical instruments as well as most dance forms. She has also worked with some of the great dance teachers of our time.

Today Twyla Tharp is known as one of America's _____ choreographers. A choreographer is a person who creates dance movements. Tharp's dances are often greeted with applause and bouquets. She has given pleasure to millions of dance lovers.

Learn More About Dance

>>>> *On a separate piece of paper or in your notebook or journal, complete the activity below.*

Appreciating Diversity

In many cultures, dance isn't just for fun. It can be a celebration or part of an important ceremony. Research the history of a dance from another country. Explain what you learn to your class. If possible, let the class see the dance or hear the music to which the dance is performed.

3 UPSKIING

In winter, some people enjoy downhill skiing. After taking ski lifts to the top of snow-covered slopes, these skiers look forward to their thrilling and challenging descents. Other people prefer the less dangerous sport of cross-country skiing. Gliding along on mostly flat terrain, these skiers enjoy calmly viewing the wintery scene.

Some skiers seek the greater challenge of skiing down very high, very remote, and very dangerous mountains. They do not, however, enjoy the hours it takes them to climb to the summits. These venturesome people have been trying out a new sport called upskiing. Upskiers use expensive, custom-made parachutes to get to mountain peaks. Once there, the skiers fold their parachutes into backpacks and ski down the slope.

Intrigued by this unusual sport, a television crew went to film upskiers on Wrangell Mountain in eastern Alaska. This mountain is known for its raging storms, dangerous crevasses, and zero visibility. An air taxi took the crew to a glacier at 9,000 feet. Although the summit was only 5,163 feet above them, the crew had to wait for 15 days until the weather was just right. Finally, a good breeze came and the skies cleared. The skiers were ecstatic. They were now able to ski uphill at 3.5 miles per hour to reach their mountain-peak destination!

MAKE A LIST

>>>> *There are eight vocabulary words in this lesson. In the story, they are boxed in color. Copy the vocabulary words here.*

1. _____
2. _____
3. _____
4. _____

5. _____
6. _____
7. _____
8. _____

MAKE AN ALPHABETICAL LIST

>>>> *Here are the eight words you copied on the previous page. Write them in alphabetical order in the spaces below.*

descents	expensive	terrain	intrigued
remote	visibility	venturesome	ecstatic

1. _____

2. _____

3. _____

4. _____

5. _____

6. _____

7. _____

8. _____

WHAT DO THE WORDS MEAN?

>>>> *Following are some meanings, or definitions, for the eight vocabulary words in this lesson. Write the words next to their definitions.*

1. _____ costly; high-priced

2. _____ interested; aroused by curiosity

3. _____ faraway; unsettled

4. _____ downward passages

5. _____ the ground

6. _____ ability to see

7. _____ very happy or joyful

8. _____ seeking adventure; daring; bold

PHONICS: Consonants

>>>> There are 26 letters in the alphabet. Twenty-one letters including the letter *y* are called consonants. Five letters (*a, e, i, o, u*) and sometimes *y* are called vowels.

Consonants appear at the beginning, at the end, and in the middle of words. Consonants that appear in the middle are called medial consonants. For example, in the word *hammer,*

h	is a beginning consonant
mm	are the medial consonants
r	is a final consonant

>>>> Here are ten words. See how well you can recognize the beginning, medial, and final consonants. Each word in the list contains consonants. Some have beginning consonants. Some have medial consonants. Some have final consonants. Some may have all three types of consonants.

>>>> ***Check each word for all three consonant positions. Then write the consonants in each word in the correct list. The first one has been done as an example.***

	Beginning	Medial	Final
1. kitten	k	tt	n
2. hoped			
3. actor			
4. corner			
5. each			
6. dancing			
7. disco			
8. umpire			

>>>> A **synonym** is a word that means the same, or nearly the same, as another word. *Happy* and *glad* are synonyms.

>>>> *The column on the left contains the eight key words in the story. To the right of each key word are three other words or groups of words. Two of these are synonyms for the key word. Circle the two synonyms.*

1. **descents**	downward passages	mountains	ways down
2. **terrain**	land	ground	climate
3. **remote**	populated	faraway	unsettled
4. **venturesome**	scared	bold	daring
5. **expensive**	costly	high priced	cheap
6. **intrigued**	interested	curious	uninterested
7. **visibility**	what can be seen	air pressure	ability to view
8. **ecstatic**	very joyful	sad	extremely happy

>>>> *These five sentences have been scrambled or mixed up. Write the words in the correct order so that they make complete sentences.*

1. popular winter is sport a skiing

_____

2. to upskiers mountain parachutes use help peaks reach

_____

3. parachutes descents tucked backpacks the are into for

_____

4. breeze needed to parachutes work a is for the strong

_____

5. most only skiers enjoy the upskiing daring

_____

USE YOUR OWN WORDS

>>>> *Look at the picture. What words come into your mind other than the ones you just matched with their synonyms? Write them on the lines below. To help you get started, here are two good words:*

1. _____ parachute _____   5. _____

2. _____ uphill _____   6. _____

3. _____   7. _____

4. _____   8. _____

COMPLETE THE STORY

>>>> Here are the eight vocabulary words for this lesson:

descents	expensive	terrain	intrigued
remote	visibility	venturesome	ecstatic

>>>> *There are four blank spaces in the story below. Four vocabulary words have already been used in the story. They are underlined. Use the other four words to fill in the blanks.*

It's good to know that there are some new sports that people are just discovering. Upskiing is one of them.

Even in the 1990s, there are mountains that have never been skied down. These mountains are usually far from cities, in _____ areas. Upskiers are <u>intrigued</u> by the challenges that these mountains present. The slopes are often ice covered with deep crevasses. The fog can be so thick that the _____ is zero. Upskiers risk their lives traveling to the mountain peaks and then skiing down the rugged <u>terrain</u>.

To reach the mountain peaks, these <u>venturesome</u> skiers use specially made, <u>expensive</u> parachutes. When a strong breeze comes and helps lift them up the mountain, the skiers feel _____. Some skiers enjoy going up mountains more than they enjoy the _____.

Learn More About Skiing

>>>> *On a separate piece of paper or in your notebook or journal, complete one or more of the activities below.*

Broadening Your Understanding
People who are active in very cold weather have to be careful. Research the health problems that can occur in the mountains in winter. Write about the dangers these adventurers face. Then write some advice you would give them about being safe during their activity.

Learning Across the Curriculum
Avalanches are one danger that winter sports-lovers face. Find out what causes an avalanche. Explain the process to your class. Make a diagram to show to the class during your presentation.

4 AN AMERICAN FIRST

Many politicians have had simple childhoods. Many have had to work their way through school. Why, then, is L. Douglas Wilder unusual? He is the first African American governor of Virginia and the first African American governor in the United States.

Wilder was born in 1931 in Richmond, the **capital** of Virginia. His parents worked hard, and the family was not rich. In fact, his grandparents had been slaves. Wilder finished college and fought in the Korean War in the early 1950s. He **objected** when the African American members of his **outfit** did not receive promotions. Shortly afterward, African Americans, including Wilder, began to receive promotions. After his time in the army, he went to law school and became a successful Richmond lawyer.

He went into politics in the early 1970s, during the civil rights movement in Virginia. Remembering his army days, he often spoke out angrily about the **limits** that blocked African Americans in his state.

Wilder's personality has seemed to **undergo** a change in the past few years. He is interested in working with his **opponents.** He is **hailed** as a person who can make good things happen. He serves as a fine **example** for others who want to serve their country.

MAKE A LIST

>>>> *There are eight vocabulary words in this lesson. In the story, they are boxed in color. Copy the vocabulary words here.*

1. _____   5. _____

2. _____   6. _____

3. _____   7. _____

4. _____   8. _____

>>>> *Here are the eight words you copied on the previous page. Write them in alphabetical order in the spaces below.*

| capital | undergo | objected | opponents |
| outfit | hailed | limits | example |

1. _____
2. _____
3. _____
4. _____

5. _____
6. _____
7. _____
8. _____

WHAT DO THE WORDS MEAN?

>>>> *Following are some meanings, or definitions, for the eight vocabulary words in this lesson. Write the words next to their definitions.*

1. _____ praised; saluted
2. _____ to experience; to go through
3. _____ a model
4. _____ the city where government meets
5. _____ a group; a team
6. _____ spoke out against; protested
7. _____ enemies; those who disagree
8. _____ borders; stopping places

>>>> **Digraphs** are two consonants or vowels that make a single sound. They can appear at the beginning, middle, and end of words. In this lesson, you will work with beginning consonant digraphs.

Here are some examples of beginning consonant digraphs.

ch	sh	kn	th	wh	wr
chip	**sh**ine	**kn**ew	**th**in	**wh**en	**wr**ong
child	**sh**oe	**kn**ife	**th**is	**wh**ere	**wr**ite

>>>> *The following sentences contain incomplete words that can be completed by using a beginning consonant digraph. Read each sentence carefully. Decide which of the digraphs listed above is needed for each underlined word. Then write the digraphs next to each incomplete word. The first one has been done as an example.*

1. The wagon won't work because a **wh**eel came off.

2. How do you like my new gold _____ain_____?

3. Did your dog catch the ball you _____rew_____?

4. My toes hurt because my _____oes_____ are too tight.

5. _____ree_____ is my lucky number. Do you _____ow_____ yours?

6. No matter how hard I try, I still can't _____istle_____.

7. The juice will stay cold if you pour it into a _____ermos_____.

8. Does your family go to _____urch_____ services?

9. He had five _____ong_____ answers, so he failed the test.

10. Do you know the story of Moby Dick, the _____ite_____ _____ale_____?

>>>> A **synonym** is a word that means the same, or nearly the same, as another word. *Happy* and *glad* are synonyms.

>>>> *The column on the left contains the eight key words in the story. To the right of each key word are three other words or groups of words. Two of these are synonyms for the key word. Circle the two synonyms.*

1.	**objected**	protested	argued	agreed
2.	**limits**	borders	coverings	barriers
3.	**undergo**	receive	live through	experience
4.	**hailed**	praised	attacked	supported
5.	**capital**	governing city	largest city	government center
6.	**example**	action	model	sample
7.	**opponents**	enemies	friends	rivals
8.	**outfit**	group	outing	team

>>>> There are many words in our language that are often misspelled. These words are spelled incorrectly so many times that they are sometimes called *spelling demons*. (A demon is a devil, or an evil spirit, and these words cause a great deal of trouble.)

>>>> *Here are some words that cause trouble. There is a correct spelling and an incorrect one. Underline the correct spelling. Then write out each correct word on the blank lines. The first one has been done as an example.*

Correct Spelling

<u>receive</u>	recieve	receive
sucess	success	_____
pleasant	pleasent	_____
certain	certin	_____
seperate	separate	_____
benefit	benifit	_____
discribe	describe	_____

USE YOUR OWN WORDS

>>>> *Look at the picture. What words come into your mind other than the ones you just matched with their synonyms? Write them on the lines below. To help you get started, here are two good words:*

1. _____ceremony_____   5. _____

2. _____governor_____   6. _____

3. _____   7. _____

4. _____   8. _____

COMPLETE THE STORY

>>>> Here are the eight vocabulary words for this lesson:

capital	undergo	objected	opponents
outfit	hailed	limits	example

>>>> *Four vocabulary words have been used in the story below. They are underlined. Use the four other vocabulary words to fill in the blanks.*

L. Douglas Wilder is proud of his Virginia background. Wilder was born in the _____ of Virginia. His childhood was not easy. He learned early about the _____ placed on African American people. When he joined the army, he faced another problem. He <u>objected</u> when African Americans were not given promotions. His commanding officer agreed with him. He and other members of his army _____ were given promotions after his complaints.

Wilder is a flexible politician. He is willing to <u>undergo</u> changes in his approach to government. He used to argue with his enemies, but he has learned to cooperate with his _____. This new attitude gets things done. His willingness to work with others has been <u>hailed</u> by many people. He is an <u>example</u> of the new politician whom others will copy.

Learn More About Politicians

>>>> *On a separate piece of paper or in your notebook or journal, complete one or more of the activities below.*

Broadening Your Understanding

Research the issues that people in your community feel are important. Then imagine you are running for public office in your area. What issues will you focus on? Write your campaign platform in which you tell people what you will do if elected.

Learning Across the Curriculum

Find out about the history of African Americans in politics in the United States. Make a time line of important events for African Americans in politics. Include such events as the year African Americans got the right to vote and the election of the first African American representative or senator.

33

34

5 HIGH FLYER

At the age of 14, Tito Gaona saw a movie. It changed his life. The movie was *Trapeze* with Burt Lancaster and Tony Curtis. *Curtis* played an *aerialist* who wanted to do the "triple." The triple is three *somersaults* in midair off a swinging *trapeze*. This movie inspired Gaona. He made up his mind to become a trapeze artist.

He practiced with his father, Vincent, a former *acrobat.* Vincent became his "catcher." The catcher is the person who grasps the flyer as he completes the movements. At the age of 18, Gaona was doing the "triple" in the circus. Only four persons had done the triple before Gaona. Two of them died from broken necks while performing.

During the *stunt,* Gaona moves at an *incredible* speed. He travels at 75 miles an hour. If Gaona lands on his neck, he could break it. He has only a *fraction* of a second to *tuck* his neck in. Then he has to land on his back in the net.

One day Gaona completed the "quadruple." His catcher caught him. But it was just practice. There were no cameras or spectators to see him do it. Someday, he'll do it under the Big Top, and thousands will be watching.

MAKE A LIST

>>>> *There are eight vocabulary words in this lesson. In the story, they are boxed in color. Copy the vocabulary words here.*

1. _____   5. _____

2. _____   6. _____

3. _____   7. _____

4. _____   8. _____

MAKE AN ALPHABETICAL LIST

>>>> *Here are the eight words you copied on the previous page. Write them in alphabetical order in the spaces below.*

trapeze	acrobat	tuck	aerialist
somersaults	fraction	stunt	incredible

1. _____   5. _____

2. _____   6. _____

3. _____   7. _____

4. _____   8. _____

WHAT DO THE WORDS MEAN?

>>>> *Following are some meanings, or definitions, for the eight vocabulary words in this lesson. Write the words next to their definitions.*

1. _____ a person who performs on a trapeze; a flyer

2. _____ full body turns, forward or backward

3. _____ to pull in; to draw in closely

4. _____ a daring trick; a display of skill

5. _____ a small part; less than a second in time

6. _____ a short horizontal bar, hung by two ropes, on which aerialists perform

7. _____ a skilled gymnast; an expert in tumbling

8. _____ almost impossible to believe

>>>> Once again, let's look at some words that have short vowel sounds. For example, *cap, hop, rip*. Now add *e* to each of these words. Look at the new words: *cape, hope, ripe*. Notice that each of the new words now has the *long* vowel in the middle and the final *e* is silent. A silent *e* at the end of a one-syllable word makes the vowel long.

>>>> *Here is a list of words containing the short vowel sound. Make new words by adding an e to the end of each word. Then write the new words on the lines provided. Pronounce each new word to yourself. It should have the long vowel sound. The first one has been done as an example.*

cop	cope	hug	
pip		strip	
past		cut	
pan		fad	
dim		hop	
slop		pin	
cub		rat	
kit		rid	
mad		spin	
bit		fat	

>>>> A **synonym** is a word that means the same, or nearly the same, as another word. *Happy* and *glad* are synonyms.

>>>> *The column on the left contains the eight key words in the story. To the right of each key word are three other words or groups of words. Two of these are synonyms for the key word. Circle the two synonyms.*

1. **incredible**	amazing	unbelievable	ordinary
2. **somersaults**	circus foods	acrobatic tricks	full body turns
3. **tuck**	to unfold	to pull in	to draw together
4. **aerialist**	a circus flyer	a ringmaster	a performer on a trapeze
5. **stunt**	a clever trick	a stupid idea	a daring feat
6. **acrobat**	an expert gymnast	a skilled tumbler	an animal trainer
7. **trapeze**	a circular cage	a swing for aerialists	a bar hung from two ropes
8. **fraction**	a small part	a tiny piece	the total

>>>> Many words end in *ed*, *er*, or *ing*. These endings can change the meaning of a word or form a new word.

>>>> *Add the correct ending to the word before each sentence. Then write the new word in the blank space. Remember: sometimes you drop the final e before adding the ed, er, or ing. The first one has been done as an example.*

1. **tuck**   He ___tucked___ his neck in before hitting the net.

2. **catch**   The _____ must grasp the aerialist's forearms.

3. **watch**   Someday, he will succeed, and thousands will be _____.

4. **move**   The aerialist is _____ through the air at an incredible speed.

5. **complete**   To date, no one has _____ the quadruple in public.

6. **change**   The movie *Trapeze* _____ his life.

7. **announce**   The _____ asked the crowd to be quiet.

8. **somersault**   Maria felt wonderful as she _____ through the air.

USE YOUR OWN WORDS

>>>> *Look at the picture. What words come into your mind other than the ones you just matched with their synonyms? Write them on the lines below. To help you get started, here are two good words:*

1. _____ropes_____   5. _____

2. _____flying_____   6. _____

3. _____   7. _____

4. _____   8. _____

>>>> Here are the eight vocabulary words for this lesson:

| aerialist | trapeze | tuck | incredible |
| stunt | somersaults | acrobat | fraction |

>>>> *There are four blank spaces in the story below. Four vocabulary words have already been used in the story. They are underlined. Use the other four words to fill in the blanks.*

There are many popular circus acts. Each has its own special appeal. But when an <u>aerialist</u> starts to climb to the _____, all the other acts stop. These high flyers become the center of all eyes. Even though there is a net below, the risk is still there. Flying through the air at an _____ speed does not allow for errors. A failure to <u>tuck</u> in one's head can cause serious injury.

One of the most amazing performers is Tito Gaona. He has made the triple a regular part of his act. Now he is working on the quadruple. It is not just an ordinary <u>stunt</u>. This stunt involves four back _____ in midair. Only the most skilled <u>acrobat</u> could think of trying it. It requires skill, strength, and timing. If the flyer is only a _____ off the mark, it can mean a rough tumble to the net—and more practice!

Learn More About the Circus

>>>> *On a separate piece of paper or in your notebook or journal, complete one or more of the activities below.*

Broadening Your Understanding
Circuses change as people's tastes change. Find out about some acts that circuses feature and create a circus for the future. Draw a picture of your circus.

Extending Your Reading
Circuses have a long history. Read one of these books about the circus and write why you think circuses have been so popular throughout history.

The Big Show, by Felix Sutton
The Circus, by Mary Kay Phelan
Old Bet and the Start of the American Circus, by Robert McClung

Rosalyn Yalow is the second woman to win the Nobel Prize in medicine. She's a scientist from New York City. She works 80 hours a week. Yalow feels she must work harder than men to achieve success. She says, "It's a man's world." But she's trying to change that.

Yalow worked out a way to measure substances in the blood and tissue. It doesn't matter how small the substance is. Her method can measure it. This method helps detect disease early.

In college, Yalow won high honors in science. After college, she applied for a job as a teacher's aid. But she was rejected because she was a woman. Even after this defeat, she was resolved to win. She said, "I'm going to show the world a woman can succeed."

Finally, the University of Illinois admitted her to medical school. Yalow worked and studied there until graduation. Then she returned to New York City where jobs were plentiful. Yalow got a job in a hospital. There, she began her inquiries into ways to help people. That was more than 40 years ago. She's still in New York City today, working to discover more cures for disease.

Rosalyn Yalow, super scientist, is a super woman!

MAKE A LIST

>>>> *There are eight vocabulary words in this lesson. In the story, they are boxed in color. Copy the vocabulary words here.*

1. _____   5. _____

2. _____   6. _____

3. _____   7. _____

4. _____   8. _____

MAKE AN ALPHABETICAL LIST

>>>> *Here are the eight words you copied on the previous page. Write them in alphabetical order in the spaces below.*

admitted	substances	detect	resolved
achieve	plentiful	inquiries	rejected

1. _____

2. _____

3. _____

4. _____

5. _____

6. _____

7. _____

8. _____

WHAT DO THE WORDS MEAN?

>>>> *Following are some meanings, or definitions, for the eight vocabulary words in this lesson. Write the words next to their definitions.*

1. _____ to discover; to find out

2. _____ to reach a desired goal

3. _____ questions

4. _____ materials from which something is made

5. _____ determined; fixed in purpose

6. _____ refused or turned away

7. _____ more than enough; abundant

8. _____ gave permission to enroll as a student; allowed to enter

>>>> **Blends** are the sounds of two or three consonants that come together at the beginning, middle, or end of words. You will study some beginning blends in this lesson.

Here are some examples of beginning consonant blends:

bl	**br**	**cl**	**cr**	**dr**
blend	brag	clown	crook	drop
fl	**gr**	**spr**	**str**	
flag	grass	spread	stroke	

>>>> *Complete the following sentences by supplying a word that begins with a consonant blend. For example, "The synonym for happy is _____." The answer must begin with a blend. The answer is glad. The first one has been done as an example.*

1. One of the _____blades_____ on her new pair of skates was bent.

2. He tried to catch the mouse in his new _____.

3. A word that means the opposite of *back* is _____.

4. A farmer plants seeds to get a _____.

5. A circus comic is called a _____.

6. The picture was too small for the _____.

7. Before you mail a letter, make sure it has a _____.

8. She felt pretty in her new _____.

9. After the race, he looked forward to a big _____ of cold milk.

10. Our English _____ ended early today.

>>>> A **synonym** is a word that means the same, or nearly the same, as another word. *Happy* and *glad* are synonyms.

>>>> *The column on the left contains the eight key words in the story. To the right of each key word are three other words or groups of words. Two of these are synonyms for the key word. Circle the two synonyms.*

1.	**inquiries**	questions	motions	investigations
2.	**detect**	to find out	to hate	to discover
3.	**rejected**	lost	turned away	refused
4.	**achieve**	to do well	to fail	to reach a goal
5.	**plentiful**	few	more than enough	a great many
6.	**admitted**	accepted	refused	allowed in
7.	**substances**	materials	kinds of matter	thoughts
8.	**resolved**	changed	decided	determined

>>>> **Antonyms** are words that are opposite in meaning. For example, *good / bad* and *fast / slow* are antonyms. Below are antonyms for six of the vocabulary words.

>>>> *See if you can find the vocabulary words and write them in the blank spaces on the left. The first one has been done as an example.*

Vocabulary Word	**Antonym**
1. resolved	undecided
2. _____	fail
3. _____	scarce
4. _____	accepted
5. _____	refused entrance
6. _____	answers

>>>> *Look at the picture. What words come into your mind other than the ones you just matched with their synonyms? Write them on the lines below. To help you get started, here are two good words:*

1. _____ handshake _____   5. _____

2. _____ medals _____   6. _____

3. _____   7. _____

4. _____   8. _____

>>>> Here are the eight vocabulary words for this lesson:

achieve	inquiries	detect	rejected
resolved	substances	admitted	plentiful

>>>> *There are four blank spaces in the story below. Four vocabulary words have already been used in the story. They are underlined. Use the other four words to fill in the blanks.*

Marie Curie was the first woman to win the Nobel Prize for her medical <u>inquiries</u>. That happened in 1911. Sixty-six years later, the prize was awarded to Rosalyn Yalow. She had found a new way of measuring _____ in the blood. Any discovery that can <u>detect</u> disease early deserves a prize. Many lives have been saved because of Yalow's work.

Yalow came from a poor family. But her parents _____ that their daughter would have a better life. They knew the importance of education. Yalow never forgot their advice. She was determined to <u>achieve</u> results.

After college, Yalow applied to many universities to be a teacher's aid. She was <u>rejected</u> because she was a woman. Finally, the University of Illinois _____ her. Later she returned to New York for a job. Jobs were _____ at that time.

Learn More About Nobel Prizes

>>>> *On a separate piece of paper or in your notebook or journal, complete one or more of the activities below.*

Learning Across the Curriculum
Research the discoveries of a scientist who has won a Nobel prize. Then explain to your class why the scientist earned the award and how his or her research has helped people.

Broadening Your Understanding
Imagine you are on the committee that will decide the winner of this year's Nobel Peace Prize. Decide who you believe deserves the award for this year. Write a speech explaining why you are nominating this person. You may want to do some research to gather reasons why this person deserves the award.

7 WALKING HIGH STEEL

"Look out! Steel beam coming up!" the **foreman** called. Jim Tallchief climbed the steel structure with the **skill** of a cat. Quickly, he worked his way from beam to beam. He balanced himself with **ease.** Tallchief was **alert.** He grasped the rising beam and fastened it in place.

Jim Tallchief is a Mohawk, a member of the Iroquois nation. He is proud of his Native American ancestry. Because they are so sure-footed, Mohawks are the most **agile** steelworkers in the world. Much of their labor is done in small groups. The work is very dangerous, so it is important that they cooperate with one another. Each member of the group must know that the other members will be alert under pressure.

In 1907, a bridge **collapsed** before it was finished. It caused the death of 35 Mohawks. Many women became **widows.** Strangely enough, the risk made the work more attractive to some of the Native Americans. But large groups no longer work on the same dangerous **construction** project. Now one accident cannot cause harm to so many people.

The life of a steelworker is hard. The workers are proud of their deeds. They feel that to excel on the high beam is to prove oneself.

MAKE A LIST

>>>> *There are eight vocabulary words in this lesson. In the story, they are boxed in color. Copy the vocabulary words here.*

1. _____
2. _____
3. _____
4. _____
5. _____
6. _____
7. _____
8. _____

MAKE AN ALPHABETICAL LIST

>>>> *Here are the eight words you copied on the previous page. Write them in alphabetical order in the spaces below.*

alert	construction	collapsed	agile
widows	skill	foreman	ease

1. _____   5. _____

2. _____   6. _____

3. _____   7. _____

4. _____   8. _____

WHAT DO THE WORDS MEAN?

>>>> *Following are some meanings, or definitions, for the eight vocabulary words in this lesson. Write the words next to their definitions.*

1. _____ broke down suddenly; fell down

2. _____ quick in thought and action; watchful

3. _____ the process of building

4. _____ women whose husbands have died

5. _____ having quick, easy movements; limber

6. _____ the ability to use one's knowledge in doing something

7. _____ a person in charge of a group of workers; a boss

8. _____ a natural way or manner

52

>>>> Words have rhythm. They are divided into syllables like musical beats in a song or dance. If you understand syllables, your spelling and pronunciation will improve. Say the following words slowly and clap for each syllable as you say them.

climb	=	one syllable
climb ing	=	two syllables
po ta to	=	three syllables
im poss i ble	=	four syllables

Here is a short rule to keep in mind. For each syllable, there must be a vowel sound.

>>>> *Look at the following list of words. Write the number of vowels in each word. Then say the word and listen for the number of vowel sounds. The number of vowel sounds you hear will be the number of syllables in the word. The first one has been done as an example.*

	Number of Vowels	Vowel Sounds	Syllables
drive	2	1	1
suitcase			
microfilm			
motorcycle			
football			
track			
basketball			
runner			

>>>> A **synonym** is a word that means the same, or nearly the same, as another word. *Happy* and *glad* are synonyms.

>>>> *The column on the left contains the eight key words in the story. To the right of each key word are three other words or groups of words. Two of these are synonyms for the key word. Circle the two synonyms.*

1. **foreman**	a boss	an assistant	a person in charge
2. **skill**	ability	knowledge	fear
3. **ease**	comfort	stress	relaxation
4. **alert**	lazy	watchful	quick in thought
5. **collapsed**	gave way	fell down	held together
6. **construction**	the process of building	a style of painting	a manner of building
7. **agile**	coordinated	clumsy	quick
8. **widows**	women who lost their husbands through death	divorced women	women whose husbands have died

>>>> Some words are often confused because they look alike or sound alike. For example, *there*/*their* and *where*/*wear* are often confused.

>>>> *Place the correct word in each of the blank spaces in the following sentences.*

1. **picture, pitcher**   In my baseball scrapbook, I have a
_____ of my favorite
_____.

2. **lose, loose**   Because my top button is _____,
I will probably _____ it.

3. **wait, weight**   The woman had to _____ in
line before the doctor could check her
_____.

4. **would, wood**   If we started to chop now, we _____
have enough _____ for the
entire winter.

5. **passed, past**   For the _____ three years, I
have _____ every examination
that has come my way.

6. **meat, meet**   Tell your mother I will _____ her in
front of the _____ counter.

>>>> *Look at the picture. What words come into your mind other than the ones you just matched with their synonyms? Write them on the lines below. To help you get started, here are two good words:*

1. _____water_____   5. _____

2. _____height_____   6. _____

3. _____   7. _____

4. _____   8. _____

>>>> Here are the eight vocabulary words for this lesson:

widows	construction	agile	foreman
skill	collapsed	ease	alert

>>>> *There are four blank spaces in the story below. Four vocabulary words have already been used in the story. They are underlined. Use the other four words to fill in the blanks.*

Steelworkers are special people. It takes unusual <u>skill</u> and courage to walk high beams. If one is not <u>alert</u>, lives may be in danger. Among the most _____ steelworkers are Mohawks. They have been doing this work for many years. When a high bridge is under <u>construction</u>, the _____ looks for workers he can rely on. They must be surefooted and dependable. They must also cooperate with <u>ease</u>.

Work on high beams is not without great loss. In 1907, a bridge _____ and caused the death of 35 Mohawks. This left many women as _____. This disaster did not stop the others from working. But now, smaller groups work on dangerous projects. An accident will not cause many brave people to be lost.

Learn More About Native Americans

>>>> *On a separate piece of paper or in your notebook or journal, complete one or more of the activities below.*

Working Together

Have each member of your group research the location of an Indian tribe's land. Find out the kinds of activities that were important to the people. Then have the group make a map showing the locations of the different tribes. Each member should explain to the class how the people's activities are related to the geographic area where they lived.

Learning Across the Curriculum

Use a copy of a state map to locate and identify the Native American reservations in your state or a state in which you are interested. Find out who lives on the reservations and what percentage of the state's land belongs to the Native Americans.

8 BORN TO WRITE

Gary Soto knows the meaning of poverty. He knows what it is like to grow up in a world filled with hardship. Soto grew up in California. For a while, his home was the world of migrant farm workers. He worked as a field hand. He put in long hours *harvesting* crops. Like other field hands, he was paid low wages. Also like other farm workers, his family was poor. They could not *afford* a nice home or new clothes. They often had to *accept* charity to get by.

Today Soto writes about his past. His books and poems often tell about things that really happened to him. One of his stories is about a boy who wore an ugly *jacket* to school. The boy was *ashamed* of the jacket. The color *reminded* him of dark green mush. But his mother said he had to wear it. The boy felt so bad that he got a D on a math test. He was so *upset* he even forgot the names of the state capitals.

Through his writings, Soto shows readers what it is like to be a Mexican American. He gives readers a view of what many Chicanos *experience* in fields and factories. These views are not often written about. They are not a part of the world seen on television and in the daily news. However, they are about real people who know that Gary Soto speaks honestly.

MAKE A LIST

>>>> *There are eight vocabulary words in this lesson. In the story, they are boxed in color. Copy the vocabulary words here.*

1. _____   5. _____

2. _____   6. _____

3. _____   7. _____

4. _____   8. _____

59

MAKE AN ALPHABETICAL LIST

>>>> *Here are the eight words you copied on the previous page. Write them in alphabetical order in the spaces below.*

harvesting	ashamed	accept	jacket
upset	afford	experience	reminded

1. _____   5. _____

2. _____   6. _____

3. _____   7. _____

4. _____   8. _____

WHAT DO THE WORDS MEAN?

>>>> *Following are some meanings, or definitions, for the eight vocabulary words in this lesson. Write the words next to their definitions.*

1. _____ embarrassed; feeling shame

2. _____ distressed; disturbed

3. _____ thought of something again

4. _____ gathering of crops

5. _____ the act of living through an event

6. _____ to have the ability to purchase something

7. _____ short coat

8. _____ to agree to take or receive

>>>> When you join one whole word with another whole word, a new single word is formed. This new word is called a **compound word**. For example, when you put the two words *air* and *plane* together, you get *airplane*. Here are three more examples.

steam + ship =	steamship
bed + room =	bedroom
cow + boy =	cowboy

>>>> *Draw lines from Column A to Column B to form new compound words.*

A	B
head	stick
wish	berry
drum	bow
bath	ache
blue	cut
news	bone
rain	paper
hair	tub
hard	flake
snow	sick
some	time
home	ship

>>>> A **synonym** is a word that means the same, or nearly the same, as another word. *Happy* and *glad* are synonyms.

>>>> *The column on the left contains the eight key words in the story. To the right of each key word are three other words or groups of words. Two of these are synonyms for the key word. Circle the two synonyms.*

1.	**jacket**	short coat	pocket	outer covering
2.	**accept**	refuse	receive	agree to take
3.	**ashamed**	embarrassed	proud	full of shame
4.	**experience**	beginning	past	life events
5.	**harvesting**	planting	picking	gathering
6.	**afford**	able to buy	sell	purchase
7.	**upset**	distressed	disturbed	calm
8.	**reminded**	remembered	forgot	thought about again

>>>> Many times two words are shortened into one by leaving out one or more letters and putting in an apostrophe. The shortened word is called a **contraction.** For example, *I'll* is the contraction for *I will. Don't* is the contraction for *do not.*

>>>> *In the left-hand column are the two words that form the contraction. Write the contraction in the right-hand column.*

Contraction

1. they are _____

2. you are _____

3. does not _____

4. who is _____

5. you have _____

6. it is _____

7. you will _____

8. have not _____

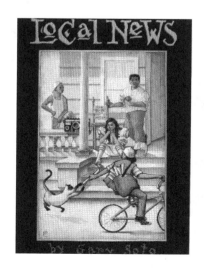

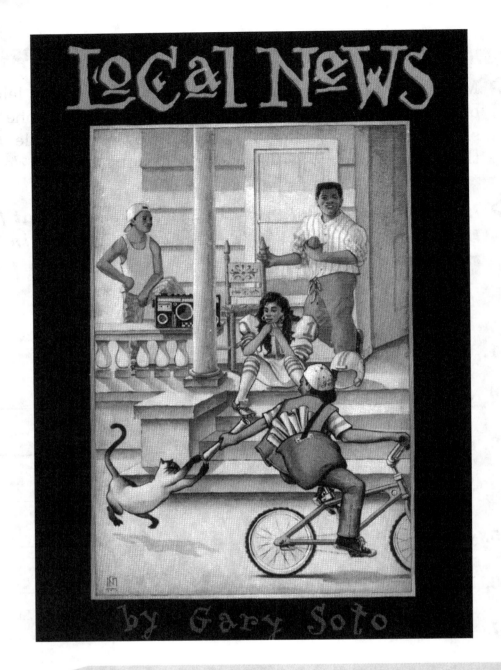

LOCAL NEWS

by Gary Soto

USE YOUR OWN WORDS

>>>> *Look at the picture. What words come into your mind other than the ones you matched with their synonyms? Write them on the lines below. To help you get started, here are two good words:*

1. _____Chicano_____   5. _____

2. _____family_____   6. _____

3. _____   7. _____

4. _____   8. _____

COMPLETE THE STORY

>>>>> Here are the eight vocabulary words for this lesson:

harvesting	ashamed	afford	upset
accept	reminded	jacket	experience

>>>>> *There are four blank spaces in the story below. Four vocabulary words have already been used in the story. They are underlined. Use the other four words to fill in the blanks.*

Gary Soto once worked as a farmhand. He spent many hours _____ crops. He received little pay for his work. He could not _____ to buy new things. Even a nice <u>jacket</u> was beyond his means!

Gary Soto is not <u>ashamed</u> of his past. He has used this _____ to become a popular author. He writes about life as a Mexican American.

Schools invite Soto to come and speak with their students. He does <u>accept</u> their invitations. He is _____ of himself when he meets Chicano children. He tells the students about his life. The students discover how <u>upset</u> Soto was living a life of poverty. But they also discover that people can make better lives for themselves. The students realize that it is possible for a poor farm worker to one day become a famous author.

Learn More About Migrant Farming

>>>>> *On a separate piece of paper or in your notebook or journal, complete one or more of the activities below.*

Appreciating Diversity

Imagine that your parents are migrant farmers. Your family has moved three times during the past year. Write a letter to a friend that describes your experiences.

Learning Across the Curriculum

The need for migrant farmers is based upon a crop's growing season. Use references to determine the growing seasons of a few states. Make a travel schedule for a farmer who wants to work all 12 months of the year. Write the time of year, identify the states the farmer should go to, and list the types of crops the farmer would be working with.

9 THE GREY CUP

The United States has the Super Bowl. Canada has the Grey Cup. Both games are lively. Without *debating* the good points of each, most people agree that the Grey Cup *arouses* more interest. The whole country takes part. It is more than a game. People celebrate. It is a *mixture* of Mardi Gras and New Year's Eve.

The game is played *alternately* in Montreal and Toronto. These cities have large stadiums. They also have the best weather for the game. Some people call the Grey Cup "the Arctic ancestor of the Super Bowl."

The Grey Cup was given by Lord Grey. It has become the main *trophy* of Canadian football. At first, the cup was to go to the winner of the amateur football title. Then the cup was changed to a professional award. Some American players have been *imported* to play for Canadian teams.

The rivalry between East and West is *intense.* The Montreal Alouettes won the Grey Cup in 1980, 1984, and 1987. But the Edmonton Eskimos *avenged* the losses in 1988 and 1989. The competition is strong. It continues to make the Grey Cup a matter of national interest in Canada.

MAKE A LIST

>>>> *There are eight vocabulary words in this lesson. In the story, they are boxed in color. Copy the vocabulary words here.*

1. _____   5. _____

2. _____   6. _____

3. _____   7. _____

4. _____   8. _____

MAKE AN ALPHABETICAL LIST

>>>> *Here are the eight words you copied on the previous page. Write them in alphabetical order in the spaces below.*

mixture	imported	trophy	debating
arouses	alternately	avenged	intense

1. _____   5. _____

2. _____   6. _____

3. _____   7. _____

4. _____   8. _____

WHAT DO THE WORDS MEAN?

>>>> *Following are some meanings, or definitions, for the eight vocabulary words in this lesson. Write the words next to their definitions.*

1. _____ a prize, often a silver cup

2. _____ stirs up strong feelings; awakens

3. _____ a combination; something made up by mixing two or more things

4. _____ brought into a country

5. _____ very strong; severe

6. _____ discussing opposing reasons; arguing

7. _____ took revenge; got even

8. _____ taking turns; first one and then another

>>>> **Prefixes** are one or more letters attached to the beginning of a word. Prefixes have different meanings. When they join words, they change the meaning of the word. There are many prefixes in our language. A few will be discussed in this lesson. For example:

> **pre** means *"before"*
>
> **pre** + cook = precook (to cook before)

> **super** means *"more than; extra"*
>
> **super** + human = superhuman (extra special human)

> **un** means *"not; the opposite of"*
>
> **un** + happy = unhappy (not happy)

>>>> *In the following list, connect the prefix with the root word. Write the new word on the lines provided.*

Prefix	Root Word	New Word
un (not; the opposite of)	+ real	= _____
super (more than; extra)	+ highway	= _____
pre (before)	+ paid	= _____
dis (not)	+ honest	= _____
re (again; back)	+ turn	= _____
in (not)	+ complete	= _____
sub (under; below)	+ marine	= _____

FIND THE SYNONYMS

>>>> A **synonym** is a word that means the same, or nearly the same, as another word. *Happy* and *glad* are synonyms.

>>>> *The column on the left contains the eight key words in the story. To the right of each key word are three other words or groups of words. Two of these are synonyms for the key word. Circle the two synonyms.*

1. **mixture**	a combination	a discovery	a blend
2. **imported**	sent out	brought in	taken in
3. **debating**	arguing	discussing	ignoring
4. **alternately**	two at a time	in turns	one after the other
5. **intense**	very strong	dull	sharp
6. **arouses**	awakens	stirs up	calms
7. **avenged**	took revenge	cheated	got even
8. **trophy**	sad event	winning prize	silver cup

>>>> Two of the words used in the story, *trophy* and *mixture*, are nouns. Think of the trophies and mixtures you have seen or read about. What words can you use to describe them?

>>>> *List as many adjectives as you can that tell something about these nouns. The list has been started for you.*

trophy	*mixture*
1. silver	1. attractive
2. magnificent	2. interesting
3.	3.
4.	4.
5.	5.
6.	6.
7.	7.
8.	8.

USE YOUR OWN WORDS

>>>> *Look at the picture. What words come into your mind other than the ones you matched with their synonyms? Write them on the lines below. To help you get started, here are two good words:*

1. _____football_____   5. _____

2. _____game_____   6. _____

3. _____   7. _____

4. _____   8. _____

>>>> Here are the eight vocabulary words for this lesson:

trophy	avenged	arouses	imported
debating	intense	alternately	mixture

>>>> *There are four blank spaces in the story below. Four vocabulary words have already been used in the story. They are underlined. Use the other four words to fill in the blanks.*

In the United States, the Super Bowl is a major event. In Canada, the Grey Cup <u>arouses</u> even more excitement. This football game is held _____ in Toronto and Montreal. These great cities can handle the large crowds. For weeks before the game, much time is spent <u>debating</u> the quality of the teams. No one tries to hide the _____ rivalry between the teams involved.

The Grey Cup has produced outstanding games over the years. Montreal and Edmonton were the rivals in 1977 and 1978. Montreal won the _____ in 1977; Edmonton <u>avenged</u> the defeat in 1978. In both games, _____ players from American colleges played key roles. This <u>mixture</u> of Canadian and American players gives the game an added interest.

Learn More About Football

>>>> *On a separate piece of paper or in your notebook or journal, complete one or more of the activities below.*

Learning Across the Curriculum

Look at the statistics of a running back of your choice. Figure the average number of *miles* he runs in a year rushing. Or look at the statistics for a quarterback and figure the number of *miles* he has passed in one season. You can find this information in yearly sports almanacs. Ask the librarian if you need some help finding it.

Broadening Your Understanding

Find out more about Canadian football and how it differs from the U.S. version. Make a chart that explains the differences. Then write a paragraph about which game you think would be more exciting and why.

10 THE ROSETTA STONE

Imagine a message so difficult that it took 14 years to **decode!** Think of a **scholar** working day and night to learn the meanings of ancient writings. Jean François Champollion of France worked on a project of this kind for many years. The work was very difficult, but he refused to be **defeated.** The text he studied was carved on a stone found in Rosetta, Egypt. It was named the Rosetta Stone.

The stone was first found by a French **engineer.** He did not think it was important. But then an **archaeologist** found it. There were strange carvings on the stone, called hieroglyphics. These are characters in Egyptian picture writing. Birds with tall crowns, snakes, and **peculiar** figures were carved on the stone.

The **text** was written in three languages. Greek, hieroglyphics, and ancient Egyptian were on the stone. Champollion **translated** the Greek section. Then he compared the Greek words with the hieroglyphics. He also knew the Coptic language. This helped him recognize many Egyptian words. Finally, in 1828, the riddle of the Rosetta Stone was solved. Because of Champollion, scholars today can read hieroglyphics and learn the history of the ancient past.

MAKE A LIST

>>>> *There are eight vocabulary words in this lesson. In the story, they are boxed in color. Copy the vocabulary words here.*

1. _____

2. _____

3. _____

4. _____

5. _____

6. _____

7. _____

8. _____

MAKE AN ALPHABETICAL LIST

>>>> *Here are the eight words you copied on the previous page. Write them in alphabetical order in the spaces below.*

engineer	scholar	text	translated
peculiar	defeated	decode	archaeologist

1. _____   5. _____

2. _____   6. _____

3. _____   7. _____

4. _____   8. _____

WHAT DO THE WORDS MEAN?

>>>> *Following are some meanings, or definitions, for the eight vocabulary words in this lesson. Write the words next to their definitions.*

1. _____ words and sentences together; a story

2. _____ a professor; a person of learning

3. _____ conquered; beaten

4. _____ to solve a puzzle; to find an answer

5. _____ a person who studies ancient life and cultures; a scientist

6. _____ a person who builds roads and bridges; a specialist in technical fields

7. _____ strange; unusual

8. _____ put into words of a different language

76

>>>> **Suffixes** are one or more letters that are attached to the *end* of a word. They also have their own meanings and change the meaning of the new word.

There are many suffixes in our language. We will review the most common ones. Study them carefully. Let's look at some common suffixes and their meanings:

Suffix	Meaning	Word with Suffix	Meaning
ful	full; full of	hand<u>ful</u>	a hand that is full
less	not any; without	home<u>less</u>	without a home
er	a person or thing	teach<u>er</u>	a person who teaches
ish	like	child<u>ish</u>	like a child
ly	in what way	quiet<u>ly</u>	done in a quiet way

>>>> *Here are eight sentences. Read them carefully and add the correct suffix. The suffix should come from the list above.*

1. He ate the pizza slow _____.

2. That African dance is grace _____.

3. If you don't study for a test, you're fool _____.

4. Who, do you think, is a good speak _____.

5. He's liked because he's cheer _____.

6. She's usual _____ the first person in line for the bus.

7. Because their work is dangerous, many astronauts are fear _____.

8. I want to be a garden _____.

>>>> A **synonym** is a word that means the same, or nearly the same, as another word. *Happy* and *glad* are synonyms.

>>>> *The column on the left contains the eight key words in the story. To the right of each key word are three other words or groups of words. Two of these are synonyms for the key word. Circle the two synonyms.*

1. **peculiar**	ordinary	strange	odd
2. **engineer**	technical director	weapon carrier	bridge designer
3. **decode**	to send a message	to translate	to solve a puzzle
4. **defeated**	overcame	seated	conquered
5. **text**	writings	words and sentences	old papers
6. **scholar**	professor	wise person	sports announcer
7. **archaeologist**	one who studies past life	one who teaches children	one who studies ancient people
8. **translated**	guessed	decoded	interpreted

>>>> There are many words in our language that are often misspelled. These words are spelled incorrectly so many times that they are sometimes called *spelling demons*. (A demon is a devil or an evil spirit—and these words cause a great deal of trouble.) Below there is a correct spelling and an incorrect one.

>>>> *Underline the correct spelling. Then write the word on the line provided. The first one has been done as an example.*

Correct Spelling

1. <u>writing</u>   writting   writing

2. athelete   athlete   _____

3. government   goverment   _____

4. interesting   intresting   _____

5. across   accross   _____

6. cafateria   cafeteria   _____

7. sandwich   sandwitch   _____

>>>> *Look at the picture. What words come into your mind other than the ones you matched with their synonyms? Write them on the lines below. To help you get started, here are two good words:*

1. _____ language _____   5. _____

2. _____ writing _____   6. _____

3. _____   7. _____

4. _____   8. _____

COMPLETE THE STORY

>>>> Here are the eight vocabulary words for this lesson:

engineer	archaeologist	translated	defeated
text	decode	scholar	peculiar

>>>> *There are four blank spaces in the story below. Four vocabulary words have already been used in the story. They are underlined. Use the other four words to fill in the blanks.*

The <u>engineer</u> tripped on a large stone. He didn't pay much attention to it. He had more important things to do, like building roads and bridges. So he threw it away. But an _____ noticed the strange carvings on the stone. These <u>peculiar</u> carvings represented Egyptian picture writing. They were called hieroglyphics. For centuries, this strange picture writing confused scientists. They just couldn't figure out what the pictures meant.

But the _____, Jean François Champollion, was determined to work it out. He would _____ these messages if it took a lifetime. He would not be _____. Actually, it was 14 years before he <u>translated</u> the writings. He found the key by comparing three different languages. Once he had solved the riddle, scientists began to work on another <u>text</u>. They could now learn the history of the past.

Learn More About Egypt

>>>> *On a separate piece of paper or in your notebook or journal, complete one or more of the activities below.*

Learning Across the Curriculum

The Rosetta Stone has the date 196 B.C. on it. Research what everyday life was like in ancient Egypt. Write about what a day would be like for a person who was living in Egypt then. If you want, draw illustrations to go with your report.

Broadening Your Understanding

Find a book about Egyptian picture writing. Write a note to a friend using this type of writing. Then have your friend write one to you. Then switch notes. Try to read what your friend wrote.

11 CRUISE CONTROL

Today Tom Cruise is a big-name movie star. He is recognized everywhere for his skill and **determination.** During the 1980s, he was ranked as one of the top five box-office stars. His performance as a Vietnam veteran in *Born on the Fourth of July* put him on the cover of *Time* magazine. It also earned him an Oscar nomination. Not bad for a boy who went to 11 different schools as he grew up! Cruise remembers **grimly,** "I was always the new kid. Always trying to fight my way to get some **attention** and love."

Cruise had other problems, too. He had a learning **disability.** He found himself in **remedial** classes in each new school. "I could never remember which way the C's and D's went," he says today.

To overcome these challenges, Cruise played sports. He was **frustrated** again and again as his family moved just as he was about to **gain** acceptance.

Finally, at the age of 17, Tom Cruise got a part in a high school production of the musical *Guys and Dolls.* "I just remember feeling so at home on stage, so **relaxed,"** he recalls. It was the beginning of his desire to be an actor. Cruise has also starred in *Risky Business, Top Gun, Rain Man, A Few Good Men,* and *Interview with a Vampire.* He seems completely at home in the movie industry.

MAKE A LIST

>>>> *There are eight vocabulary words in this lesson. In the story, they are boxed in color. Copy the vocabulary words here.*

1. _____   5. _____

2. _____   6. _____

3. _____   7. _____

4. _____   8. _____

MAKE AN ALPHABETICAL LIST

>>>> *Here are the eight words you copied on the previous page. Write them in alphabetical order in the spaces below.*

determination	attention	grimly	frustrated
disability	gain	remedial	relaxed

1. _____   5. _____

2. _____   6. _____

3. _____   7. _____

4. _____   8. _____

WHAT DO THE WORDS MEAN?

>>>> *Following are some meanings, or definitions, for the eight vocabulary words in this lesson. Write the words next to their definitions.*

1. _____ discouraged; upset by failure

2. _____ correcting

3. _____ harshly

4. _____ firmness of purpose

5. _____ care, notice

6. _____ to get; to earn

7. _____ a disadvantage; an impairment

8. _____ calm; at ease

>>>> In Lesson 3, you had practice exercises dealing with consonants. Look at the consonants again. In the alphabet, all the letters are consonants except the vowels (*a, e, i, o, u*) and sometimes *y.*

A consonant can be at the beginning of a word, in the middle of a word, or at the end of a word. For example, in the word *cabin,*

> *c* is a beginning consonant
>
> *b* is a medial consonant
>
> *n* is a final consonant

>>>> Here are ten words. See how well you can recognize the beginning, middle, and final consonants.

>>>> *After each word, write the letter* **B** *if the word contains a beginning consonant. Write* **M** *if the word contains a medial consonant. Write* **F** *if the word contains a final consonant.*

Each word on the list contains at least one consonant. Some words contain more than one consonant. The first one has been done for you.

1. read _____ B, F _____   **6.** umbrella _____

2. answer _____   **7.** writing _____

3. question _____   **8.** Olympics _____

4. book _____   **9.** use _____

5. creep _____   **10.** anybody _____

>>>> A **synonym** is a word that means the same, or nearly the same, as another word. *Happy* and *glad* are synonyms.

>>>> *The column on the left contains the eight key words in the story. To the right of each key word are three other words or groups of words. Two of these are synonyms for the key word. Circle the two synonyms.*

1.	**determination**	anger	firmness of purpose	willpower
2.	**grimly**	sadly	cheerfully	seriously
3.	**disability**	injury	handicap	clumsiness
4.	**remedial**	stupid	correcting	curing
5.	**attention**	care	worry	notice
6.	**frustrated**	discouraged	surprised	upset
7.	**gain**	to win	to earn	to help
8.	**relaxed**	tense	calm	comfortable

>>>> An **adjective** is a word that describes a person, place, or thing. For example, in the sentence "Tom Cruise is a handsome and talented actor," *handsome* and *talented* are adjectives that describe *actor*.

>>>> *Underline the adjectives in the following sentences. The first one has been done as an example.*

1. We had a long, cold wait at the theater to see the famous star.

2. His easy charm makes Tom Cruise a favorite actor.

3. Many of Cruise's younger fans try to copy his cheerful, friendly manner.

4. Even his early pictures show that he would be a special and an exciting, new talent.

5. Behind his good looks, Cruise is a careful, sensitive, and dedicated actor.

USE YOUR OWN WORDS

>>>> *Look at the picture. What words come into your mind other than the ones you matched with their synonyms? Write them on the lines below. To help you get started, here are two good words:*

1. _____ successful _____   5. _____

2. _____ confident _____   6. _____

3. _____   7. _____

4. _____   8. _____

COMPLETE THE STORY

>>>> Here are the eight vocabulary words for this lesson:

determination	attention	grimly	frustrated
disability	gain	remedial	relaxed

>>>> *There are four blank spaces in the story below. Four vocabulary words have already been used in the story. They are underlined. Use the other four words to fill in the blanks.*

Tom Cruise is someone who has overcome a _____ to reach his goal. His family moved often. He became a _____ student when he was unable to fit in at the new schools he attended so often. Other students either ignored him or thought he was not smart because he was in a _____ reading class. Cruise still remembers how hard it was to get _____ from his classmates.

Cruise worked hard to <u>gain</u> acceptance, but he was never really happy. He still talks <u>grimly</u> about his school days.

In the end, of course, his <u>determination</u> paid off. He took a part in a play and found that he felt completely <u>relaxed</u> on stage. That play was a turning point in his life.

Learn More About The Movies

>>>> *On a separate piece of paper or in your notebook or journal, complete one or more of the activities below.*

Broadening Your Understanding

Watch a movie on T.V. or in a movie theater and write a review of it. Comment on the plot, the characters, the subject, and how well the movie works. Read your movie review to the class.

Extending Your Reading

Special effects are an important part of the movies. Read one of the books below about how moviemakers create realistic characters and scenes. Present your findings to the class.

Movies F/X, by Ian Rimmer
How Movies Are Made, by Gwen Cherrell
Movie Monsters, by Tom Powers

12 A HOME-RUN HITTER

To many people, Edward James Olmos is the picture of success. He appeared in the television program "Miami Vice." He has starred in several movies. He won an Academy Award nomination for his role in the movie *Stand and Deliver*.

However, success did not come easy for Olmos. He had to work hard to become a star. Olmos grew up in a poor area of Los Angeles. Olmos looked for something to help him get through his rough childhood. He began to play baseball. He worked hard to improve his skills. He became the California batting champion. He practiced with the major league hitters.

Today Olmos says that baseball had a huge effect on his life. He learned self-discipline and patience. Baseball taught him to be determined and to keep working toward a goal. Olmos used these skills during the years when he was a struggling actor. For a long time, he was only given small parts He began a furniture delivery business to pay his bills and to support his family. He performed at night. In time, Olmos landed bigger parts. He won a Tony Award for his performance in the play *Zoot Suit*. This performance led to more offers. Olmos directed and starred in the movie *American Me*. Olmos reached his goal of stardom. He had hit a home run once again!

MAKE A LIST

>>>> *There are eight vocabulary words in this lesson. In the story, they are boxed in color. Copy the vocabulary words here.*

1. _____   5. _____
2. _____   6. _____
3. _____   7. _____
4. _____   8. _____

MAKE AN ALPHABETICAL LIST

>>>> *Here are the eight words you copied on the previous page. Write them in alphabetical order in the spaces below.*

effect	success	area	league
champion	patience	support	improve

1. _____   5. _____

2. _____   6. _____

3. _____   7. _____

4. _____   8. _____

WHAT DO THE WORDS MEAN?

>>>> *Following are some meanings, or definitions, for the eight vocabulary words in this lesson. Write the words next to their definitions.*

1. _____ to make better

2. _____ the result; something made to happen; influence

3. _____ an association of teams or clubs

4. _____ the willingness to wait; steady effort

5. _____ to provide for

6. _____ the achievement of something desired

7. _____ the winner of a contest

8. _____ a region; a section

>>>> In Lesson 1, you learned the short vowel sounds. In this lesson, you will review the short vowel sounds. Here are some examples of each of the short vowel sounds.

short ă	short ĕ	short ĭ	short ŏ	short ŭ
măp	wĕt	fĭt	mŏp	hŭt

>>>> *Read the following true story and underline the words with short vowel sounds.*

Did you read about Pinky, the circus elephant? He'd turn his head away whenever his master gave him water. He only liked to drink soda. Pinky would put his trunk into the barrel and guzzle up all the soda. He drank so fast that his trunk sucked up a lot of air. Then he'd belch and burp. All the circus people would gather and watch Pinky for their evening fun.

USING YOUR LANGUAGE: Antonyms

>>>> **Antonyms** are words that are opposite in meaning. For example, *good* and *bad* and *fast* and *slow* are antonyms. Here are antonyms for five of the vocabulary words.

>>>> *See if you can find the vocabulary words. Write them in the blank spaces on the left.*

Vocabulary Word	Antonym
1._____	restlessness
2._____	failure
3._____	decline
4._____	loser
5._____	cause

93

FIND THE SYNONYMS

>>>> A **synonym** is a word that means the same, or nearly the same, as another word. *Happy* and *glad* are synonyms.

>>>> *The column on the left contains the eight key words in the story. To the right of each key word are three other words or groups of words. Two of these are synonyms for the key word. Circle the two synonyms.*

1.	**improve**	weaken	make better	increase quality
2.	**area**	region	size	section
3.	**support**	provide	abandon	take care of
4.	**patience**	restlessness	steady effort	endurance
5.	**effect**	cause	influence	result
6.	**league**	sport	association	organization
7.	**champion**	winner	one who comes in first place	contest
8.	**success**	achievement	desired outcome	loss

USE YOUR OWN WORDS

>>>> *Look at the picture. What words come into your mind other than the ones you matched with their synonyms? Write them on the lines below. To help you get started, here are two good words:*

1. _____actor_____   5. _____

2. ___demonstrating___   6. _____

3. _____   7. _____

4. _____   8. _____

95

COMPLETE THE STORY

>>>> Here are the eight vocabulary words for this lesson:

success	improve	patience	champion
support	league	area	effect

>>>> *There are four blank spaces in the story below. Four vocabulary words have already been used in the story. They are underlined. Use the other four words to fill in the blanks.*

When Edward James Olmos joined his first baseball _____ he had no idea of the <u>effect</u> the sport would have on his life! He thought the game would simply give him a way of escaping the tough _____ in which he lived. But baseball taught Olmos skills that he would use for the rest of his life. He discovered that through hard work he could <u>improve</u> his skills. He learned to keep focused on his goals. He found that with _____ and determination, he could become a <u>champion</u>.

Olmos used these same skills to become a famous actor. For years, he worked in small roles. He struggled to _____ his family, often working two jobs. His major break came when he appeared in "Miami Vice." His lead in the picture *Stand and Deliver* marked the greatest point of his journey so far. Edward James Olmos received an Academy Award nomination for the performance. <u>Success</u> was finally his!

>>>> *On a separate piece of paper or in your notebook or journal, complete one or more of the activities below.*

Building Language

Edward James Olmos's lucky break came when he appeared in the play *Zoot Suit*. Use reference texts to find out the meaning of the phrase *zoot suit*. Make a drawing of a zoot suit to share with your class.

Learning Across the Curriculum

Olmos says that baseball had a big influence on his life. Use reference texts to learn more about the origins of this sport. Find out who first created the game, where it was played, and what the original rules were. Share your findings with the class in a short speech.

Broadening Your Understanding

Many television and movie actors are Latinos. Find out about the life of one such actor. Then give a speech to your class while pretending you are that actor. Tell your classmates how you first became involved with acting, the effect it had on your life, and your motto for success.

13 BORN TO SING

There was always music in his home. His family sang for fun. They sang while they worked. When not singing, the family listened to classical music. The family's life was *focused* on music. This was the *atmosphere* in which Luciano Pavarotti grew up.

His father was a baker with the soul of a singer. He enjoyed singing at *community* meetings. He hoped his son would one day become a singer. However, Pavarotti wanted to be a professional soccer player.

His mother had *doubts* about her son's plan for the future. She convinced him to become a *primary* school teacher. Even while he taught, Pavarotti studied music and singing. When he won an important *tenor* contest, he left teaching. That same year, he made his debut in the opera *La Bohéme*. Success soon followed. He had the winning mixture of voice and looks. His handsome, *masculine* appearance won many admirers.

Today Pavarotti is considered one of the world's greatest opera stars. Televised broadcasts of his *concerts* have made him quite popular. A 1992 broadcast of his concert with José Carreras and Placido Domingo was viewed by millions of fans. The recording of this concert was the top seller in classical music that year. Through events like this, Pavarotti took classical music out of the opera house and into the living room!

MAKE A LIST

>>>> *There are eight vocabulary words in this lesson. In the story, they are boxed in color. Copy the vocabulary words here.*

1. _____   5. _____

2. _____   6. _____

3. _____   7. _____

4. _____   8. _____

MAKE AN ALPHABETICAL LIST

>>>> *Here are the eight words you copied on the previous page. Write them in alphabetical order in the spaces below.*

atmosphere	community	tenor	primary
focused	masculine	doubts	concerts

1. _____   5. _____

2. _____   6. _____

3. _____   7. _____

4. _____   8. _____

WHAT DO THE WORDS MEAN?

>>>> *Following are some meanings, or definitions, for the eight vocabulary words in this lesson. Write the words next to their definitions.*

1. _____ a male singer, often in opera

2. _____ people living together in a particular town or district; a group of people

3. _____ manly; full of strength and vigor

4. _____ concentrated; centered

5. _____ first four years of school; usually refers to kindergarten through grade 3

6. _____ an environment; a mood

7. _____ musical performances

8. _____ uncertainties; distrust

>>>> Remember: **prefixes** are one or more letters attached to the beginning of a root word. Prefixes have different meanings. When they join words they change the meaning of that word. There are many prefixes in our language. Here are a few more to help you figure out word meanings. For example:

> **auto** means "by" or "for" or "of oneself"
>
> **co** means "with" or "together"

> **de** means "away from" or "off"
>
> **mis** means "wrong" or "mistake"

> **fore** means "before" or "in front"
>
> **inter** means "between" or "among"

>>>> *In the following list, connect the prefix with the root word. Write the new word.*

Prefix		Root Word		New Word
1. fore	+	man	=	_____
2. mis	+	place	=	_____
3. inter	+	state	=	_____
4. de	+	frost	=	_____
5. auto	+	biography	=	_____
6. co	+	operate	=	_____

>>>> A **synonym** is a word that means the same, or nearly the same, as another word. *Happy* and *glad* are synonyms.

>>>> *The column on the left contains the eight key words in the story. To the right of each key word are three other words or groups of words. Two of these are synonyms for the key word. Circle the two synonyms.*

1. **community**   group of people   town of people   list of people

2. **masculine**   feminine   manly   of a male

3. **doubts**   distrust   beliefs   uncertainties

4. **primary**   early school years   grades 9-12   kindergarten through grade 3

5. **focused**   concentrated   centered   wandered

6. **atmosphere**   environment   habits   mood

7. **tenor**   singer   designer   opera star

8. **concerts**   books   musical programs   performances

>>>> **Nouns** are words used to show names of persons, places, things, actions, ideas, and qualities. There are two kinds of nouns, proper and common. **Common nouns** are names of any persons, places, or things, such as *traveler*, *city*, or *box*. **Proper nouns** are names of particular persons, places, or things, such as *Helen*, *New York City*, or *Sears Tower*.

>>>> *Underline the nouns in each of the sentences below. Place one line under each common noun. Place two lines under each proper noun.*

1. Luciano Pavarotti was born in the town of Modena in Italy.

2. His mother convinced him to be a teacher in a primary school.

3. His tour of Australia is one of his fondest memories.

4. Any opera lover can recite the great roles sung by Pavarotti.

5. Pavarotti made his debut in Italian opera as Rodolfo in La Bohème.

6. The singer loved to tell tales of his great performances at the Metropolitan Opera House.

USE YOUR OWN WORDS

>>>> *Look at the picture. What words come into your mind other than the ones you matched with their synonyms? Write them on the lines below. To help you get started, here are two good words:*

1. _____couple_____ 5. _____

2. _____hand_____ 6. _____

3. _____ 7. _____

4. _____ 8. _____

COMPLETE THE STORY

>>>> Here are the eight vocabulary words for this lesson:

focused	doubts	atmosphere	primary
community	masculine	tenor	concerts

>>>> *There are four blank spaces in the story below. Four vocabulary words have already been used in the story. They are underlined. Use the other four words to fill in the blanks.*

Pavarotti's early life was <u>focused</u> on music. However, he first became a teacher. He taught in a _____ school for two years. But he loved the <u>atmosphere</u> of opera. He continued to study music and singing. Then Pavarotti got a big break. He won an important _____ contest.

His debut was in the Italian opera *La Bohéme*. After this performance, there were no _____ that Pavarotti was destined for stardom. He had just the right combination of voice and _____ good looks. He was invited to appear at the world's most famous opera houses. Millions of people viewed his televised <u>concerts</u>. He gained great respect in the special <u>community</u> of opera singers. Many people regard Pavarotti as one of the greatest opera singers ever.

Learn More About Opera

>>>> *On a separate piece of paper or in your notebook or journal, complete one or more of the activities below.*

Learning Across the Curriculum

Opera has a long history. Find out something about the history of this art form. Write a short history of the opera. Include why it was first created and who some of the major singers in the history of opera are. Also include information about some of the most famous composers of opera.

Broadening Your Understanding

Arias are the solo songs of opera. Go to the library and listen to some arias. (Mozart and Wagner wrote many arias). Then write a paragraph about these songs. How are the arias you listened to alike? How are they different?

106

14 SHOOTING BACK

Photographer Jim Hubbard *explores* people's lives through his camera. He wanted to find out more about people who are homeless. He took pictures of some children as they played. One of them was a boy named Dion.

Dion and his family lived in a *hotel* in Washington, DC. Hubbard took pictures of the family. He found that Dion's family was just like other families. Only one thing was different. Dion's family did not have a home.

Dion showed Hubbard some pictures he had taken. Hubbard taught Dion how to take better pictures. Other children asked Hubbard if they could take pictures. Hubbard couldn't help all the kids by himself. He asked other photographers to volunteer their time. The adults gave classes at homeless *shelters.* Many of the children's pictures were *collected.* They were put on *exhibit.* Some photos were used in a book.

The exhibit *resulted* in a *program* called Shooting Back. This program is for homeless children. It helps them express themselves through pictures. It gives them a *sense* of pride. The program also teaches people about the homeless. The pictures show that homeless children are like other children.

MAKE A LIST

>>>> *There are eight vocabulary words in this lesson. In the story, they are boxed in color. Copy the vocabulary words here.*

1. _____   5. _____

2. _____   6. _____

3. _____   7. _____

4. _____   8. _____

107

MAKE AN ALPHABETICAL LIST

>>>> *Here are the eight words you copied on the previous page. Write them in alphabetical order in the spaces below.*

collected	shelters	exhibit	program
sense	explores	resulted	hotel

1. _____   5. _____

2. _____   6. _____

3. _____   7. _____

4. _____   8. _____

WHAT DO THE WORDS MEAN?

>>>> *Following are some meanings, or definitions, for the eight vocabulary words in this lesson. Write the words next to their definitions.*

1. _____ to place an object or collection of objects on show

2. _____ public housing

3. _____ gathered

4. _____ organized activities

5. _____ a feeling or impression

6. _____ studies; examines

7. _____ happened because of something

8. _____ places that give cover or protection

>>>> In Lesson 4, you learned about beginning digraphs. Now, you're going to learn about digraphs at the *end* of words.

Let's review. **Digraphs** are two consonant sounds that make a single sound. For example:

<u>wh</u> as in <u>wh</u>en (beginning digraph)

<u>sh</u> as in wa<u>sh</u> (final digraph)

<u>ch</u> as in pit<u>ch</u> (final digraph)

Here are some more examples of final digraphs:

ch	sh	gh	ph	th	ck	gn
ea<u>ch</u>	bru<u>sh</u>	cou<u>gh</u>	gra<u>ph</u>	wi<u>th</u>	ba<u>ck</u>	si<u>gn</u>

>>>> *Underline the words in the story below that contain consonant digraphs at the end of words.*

Did you ever wish that you could be an actor? Then you could autograph your photograph and laugh with your fans. You might design a new ranch or a French house. You could watch your own movies or wash your face in a marble bath.

You might choose to play a tough guy. If you practice enough, you should get a chance to sing. Be sure you brush up both skills. If you are picked for a major movie role, you will want to do it right.

FIND THE SYNONYMS

>>>> A **synonym** is a word that means the same, or nearly the same, as another word. *Happy* and *glad* are synonyms.

>>>> *The column on the left contains the eight key words in the story. To the right of each key word are three other words or groups of words. Two of these are synonyms for the key word. Circle the two synonyms.*

1. **explores**	leaves	searches	investigates
2. **hotel**	public housing	apartment	temporary home
3. **sense**	feeling	hearing	impression
4. **exhibit**	display	show	leave
5. **shelters**	places that provide protection	safe places	open areas
6. **collected**	spread out	gathered	brought together
7. **resulted**	ended	began	followed
8. **program**	planned events	directions	organized system

>>>> Many times two words are shortened into one by leaving out one or more letters and putting in an apostrophe. The shortened word is called a **contraction.** For example, *I'll* is the contraction for *I will*. *Don't* is the contraction for *do not*.

>>>> *In the left column are some common contractions. Write the two words the contraction stands for in the right column.*

Contraction	Words Contraction Stands For
1. we'll	_____
2. he'll	_____
3. wouldn't	_____
4. hadn't	_____
5. we're	_____
6. I'm	_____

USE YOUR OWN WORDS

>>>> *Look at the picture. What words come into your mind other than the ones you matched with their synonyms? Write them on the lines below. To help you get started, here are two good words:*

1. _____photography_____   5. _____

2. _____homeless_____   6. _____

3. _____   7. _____

4. _____   8. _____

>>>> Here are the eight vocabulary words for this lesson:

exhibit	explores	shelters	hotels
sense	collected	program	resulted

>>>> *There are four blank spaces in the story below. Four vocabulary words have already been used in the story. They are underlined. Use the other four words to fill in the blanks.*

Shooting Back is a _____ designed to help homeless children. Professional photographers volunteer to teach the youngsters how to take photographs. They hold workshops at homeless <u>shelters</u> and sometimes at <u>hotels</u> where poor people are given a room to stay. The adults explain how to use a camera. They teach the children how to take good pictures.

The children are given cameras. They are encouraged to express themselves. Each child <u>explores</u> the world through a camera's lens. The pictures the children take are _____ and put on _____ .

For the children, the Shooting Back program <u>resulted</u> in a _____ of pride in what they did. They felt good about themselves and their accomplishments. They also were able to show others what their homeless world is like.

Learn More About Homelessness

>>>> *On a separate piece of paper or in your notebook or journal, complete one or more of the activities below.*

Learning Across the Curriculum

Use reference books to find out the number of homeless people estimated to live in your state. Then determine the homeless population in four other states. Display your findings in a graph.

Broadening Your Understanding

Homelessness is a problem that affects all members of our society. Contact a local homeless shelter in your town. Find out what you can do to help these people. Make a poster that encourages your classmates to help out, too.

15 SAN GENNARO

New York would not be the same without the Festival of San Gennaro. Once a year along Mulberry Street in New York City, there is a feast. The festival is a ten-block **spectacle.** People come to eat, drink, sing, and dance. Everyone is friendly. There are hundreds of booths in the streets. They **overflow** with all kinds of Italian food.

For at least a **generation,** people have honored San Gennaro. He was a third-century bishop. It is said that his prayers saved Naples by stopping a huge volcanic **eruption.**

During the feast, the saint's **bust** is draped in red ribbons. It is carried through the streets of Little Italy, an area in New York City that is primarily Italian. A service is held in honor of the saint. Then the statue is taken to a shrine where it has the place of honor.

The feast lasts 11 days. Every night is **exciting.** There are many arches aglow with the light of 2 million bulbs. Musicians play love songs. The air is filled with **romance.** After watching street dances, people eat and enjoy themselves until they are **weary.** Everyone is welcome at the San Gennaro Festival. Perhaps you can join the fun someday.

MAKE A LIST

>>>> *There are eight vocabulary words in this lesson. In the story, they are boxed in color. Copy the vocabulary words here.*

1. _____   5. _____

2. _____   6. _____

3. _____   7. _____

4. _____   8. _____

115

MAKE AN ALPHABETICAL LIST

>>>> *Here are the eight words you copied on the previous page. Write them in alphabetical order in the spaces below.*

romance	overflow	spectacle	bust
weary	eruption	exciting	generation

1. _____   5. _____

2. _____   6. _____

3. _____   7. _____

4. _____   8. _____

WHAT DO THE WORDS MEAN?

>>>> *Following are some meanings, or definitions, for the eight vocabulary words in this lesson. Write the words next to their definitions.*

1. _____ the bursting forth of a volcano; throwing out of lava

2. _____ tired; worn out

3. _____ stirring; thrilling

4. _____ a period of time (approximately 30 years); people living during the same period of time

5. _____ an unusual sight; an elaborate show or display

6. _____ to flow or spread over

7. _____ a piece of sculpture representing the upper part of the body; a statue

8. _____ a feeling of love and adventure; affection

>>>> In Lesson 6, you were introduced to consonant blends. Remember: **Consonant blends** are made by two or three consonants coming together. They can appear at the beginning, middle, and end of words. In Lesson 6, you worked with beginning blends. Now you will work with blends at the *end* of words. For example:

st	**sk**	**ng**	**nd**	**nk**	**lf**
fea<u>st</u>	de<u>sk</u>	ba<u>ng</u>	sa<u>nd</u>	tha<u>nk</u>	se<u>lf</u>
wri<u>st</u>	fla<u>sk</u>	ra<u>ng</u>	e<u>nd</u>	ba<u>nk</u>	she<u>lf</u>

>>>> *Complete the following sentences by supplying a word that ends with a consonant blend. Use only those words that appear in the examples above. The first one has been done as an example.*

1. A synonym for *loud noise* is _____bang_____.

2. For the many favors you have done, I say "_____ you."

3. The small part of your arm above your hand is called your _____.

4. The reference books can be found on the top _____.

5. We had so many good things to eat that our meal could be called a _____.

6. Don't keep too much cash on hand. It is always better to deposit it in a _____.

7. If I don't straighten the top of my _____, I'll never find my homework.

8. I can't wait until I reach the _____ of my book.

>>>> A **synonym** is a word that means the same, or nearly the same, as another word. *Happy* and *glad* are synonyms.

>>>> *The column on the left contains the eight key words in the story. To the right of each key word are three other words or groups of words. Two of these are synonyms for the key word. Circle the two synonyms.*

1.	**spectacle**	a spy	a display	a great show
2.	**romance**	love	affection	foolishness
3.	**overflow**	to run over	to spread over	to see over
4.	**eruption**	throwing out	slowing down	bursting forth
5.	**exciting**	stirring	puzzling	thrilling
6.	**generation**	a forgotten time	a period of time	people living in the same time period
7.	**weary**	fatigued	overjoyed	tired
8.	**bust**	a sculpture of the upper part of the body	a statue	a shelf

>>>> *In each of the following sentences, there are words that require capital letters. Rewrite each sentence so the words are correctly capitalized. Remember that capital letters are used in the following places: first word in a sentence; names of people, cars, cities, states, countries, holidays, days of the week, and months of the year.*

1. naples was saved by saint gennaro, who stopped the eruption of mount vesuvius.

_____

_____

2. every september along mulberry street in new york city, there is a festival that honors san gennaro.

_____

_____

3. if you enjoy italian food from rome and genoa, hurry to the booth at the corner of mulberry street and second avenue.

_____

_____

>>>> *Look at the picture. What words come into your mind other than the ones you matched with their synonyms? Write them on the lines below. To help you get started, here are two good words:*

1. _____grill_____   5. _____

2. _____food_____   6. _____

3. _____   7. _____

4. _____   8. _____

COMPLETE THE STORY

>>>> Here are the eight vocabulary words for this lesson:

overflow	eruption	bust	generation
weary	exciting	romance	spectacle

>>>> *There are four blank spaces in the story below. Four vocabulary words have already been used in the story. They are underlined. Use the other four words to fill in the blanks.*

You are on your way to the San Gennaro Festival. All year, you have waited for this _____ spectacle. Ahead of you is an evening of fun and food. You haven't eaten all day. You know the booths will _____ with all kinds of food. Here's your chance to sample dozens of tasty items. Just don't overdo it.

The colorful parade begins. Hundreds of people crowd around the bust of Saint Gennaro. They rush to pin dollar bills on the red ribbons. Not many people know that Saint Gennaro saved Naples by stopping the _____ of a great volcano.

Late that night, you return home. You are _____ from hours of dancing and singing. But everything was so cheerful and lovely. It was a night of romance. You are pleased that this festival is part of your generation. You hope that it will continue for many more years.

Learn More About Festivals

>>>> *On a separate piece of paper or in your notebook or journal, complete one or more of the activities below.*

Appreciating Diversity

Find out about a festival in your native country. Imagine you are walking through the festival. Write about what you think it is like to be there. What do you see? What do you hear? What do you smell?

Broadening Your Understanding

People plan festivals for everything from strawberries to saints. Go to the library and look in travel books for a book about an area you would like to visit. Then find out what festivals you might see there. Write about the festival you would most like to see.

A

accept *[AK sept]* to agree to take or receive

achieve *[uh CHEEV]* to reach a desired goal

acrobat *[AK ruh bat]* a skilled gymnast; an expert in tumbling

admitted *[ad MIT ted]* gave permission to enroll as a student; allowed to enter

aerialist *[AIR ee uh list]* a person who performs on a trapeze

afford *[uh FOHRD]* to have the ability to purchase something

agile *[AJ ul]* having quick, easy movements; limber

aid *[AYD]* to help; to give what is useful or necessary

alert *[uh LURT]* quick in thought and action; watchful

alternately *[AWL tur nit lee]* taking turns; first one and then another

appeared *[uh PEERD]* was seen (on stage or screen); performed

archaeologist *[ar kee OL uh jist]* a person who studies ancient life and cultures; a scientist

area *[AYR ee uh]* a region; a section

arouses *[uh ROUZ ez]* stirs up strong feelings; awakens

ashamed *[uh SHAYMD]* embarrassed; feeling shame

atmosphere *[AT mus feer]* an environment; a mood

attention *[uh TEN shun]* notice, care

avenged *[uh VENJD]* took revenge; got even

B

background *[BAK ground]* accompanying the main action

bouquets *[boo KAYZ]* bunches of flowers fastened together

bust *[BUST]* a piece of sculpture representing the upper part of the body; a statue

C

capital *[KAP uh tul]* the city where government meets

champion *[CHAM pee ohn]* the winner of a contest

collapsed *[kul LAPSD]* broke down suddenly; fell down

collected *[kuh LEKT uhd]* gathered

combines *[kum BYNZ]* joins together; mixes

community *[kuh MYOO nih tee]* people living together in a particular town or district; a group of people

composer *[kom POH zur]* a person who writes music

concerts *[KOHN suhrtz]* musical performances

construction *[kun STRUK shun]* the process of building

D

debating *[dih BAYT ing]* discussing opposing reasons; arguing

decode *[dee KOHD]* to solve a puzzle; to find an answer

defeated *[dih FEET id]* conquered; beaten

descents *[dee SENTS]* downward passages

detect *[dih TEKT]* to discover; to find out

determination *[dih TUR muh NAY shun]* firmness of purpose

disability *[dis uh BIL uh tee]* a disadvantage; an impairment

doubts *[DOWTS]* uncertainties; distrust

E

ease *[EEZ]* a natural way or manner

ecstatic *[ek STAT ik]* very happy or joyful

effect *[e FEKT]* the result; something made to happen; influence

engineer *[en juh NEER]* a person who builds roads and bridges; a specialist in technical fields

eruption *[ih RUP shun]* bursting forth of a volcano; throwing out of lava

example *[eg ZAM pul]* a model

exciting *[ek SY ting]* stirring; thrilling

exhibit *[eks IB it]* to place an object or collection of objects on show

expensive *[ek SPENS iv]* costly; high-priced

experience *[ek SPIHR ee uhns]* the act of living through an event

explores *[ek SPLOHRZ]* studies or examines

F

focused *[FOH kusd]* concentrated; centered

foreman *[FOR man]* a person in charge of a group of workers; a boss

fraction *[FRAK shun]* a small part; less than a second in time

frustrated *[FRUS trayt id]* discouraged; upset by failure

G

gain *[GAYN]* to get; to earn

generation *[jen uh RAY shun]* a period of time (approximately 30 years); people living during the same period of time

grand [GRAND] large; important; complete

grimly *[GRIM lee]* harshly

H

hailed *[HAYLD]* praised; saluted

harvesting *[HAHR vihs ting]* gathering of crops

hotel *[hoh TEL]* public housing

I

imported *[im PORT id]* brought into a country

improve *[im PROOV]* to make better

incredible *[in KRED uh bul]* almost impossible to believe

inquiries *[IN kwuh reez]* questions

intense *[in TENS]* very strong; severe

intrigued *[in TREEGD]* interested; aroused by curiosity

J

jacket *[JAK it]* a short coat

justice *[JUS tis]* fairness; rightfulness

L

league *[LEEG]* an association of teams or clubs

legal *[LEE gul]* having to do with the law or with lawyers

limits *[LIM its]* borders; stopping places

M

major *[MAY jor]* main; principal

masculine *[MAS kyoo lin]* manly; full of strength and vigor

mixture *[MIKS chur]* a combination; something made up by mixing two or more things

O

objected *[ob JECT id]* spoke out against; protested

opponents *[uh POH nents]* enemies; those who disagree

outfit *[OUT fit]* a group; a team

overflow *[oh vur FLOW]* to flow or spread over

P

patience *[PAY shuhns]* the willingness to wait; steady effort

peculiar *[pih KYOOL yur]* strange; unusual

123

plentiful *[PLEN tih ful]* more than enough; abundant

primary *[PRY mayr ree]* first four years of school; usually refers to kindergarten through grade 3

program *[PROH gram]* organized activities

R

rebel *[REB ul]* a person who goes against the system; one who resists authority

rejected *[rih JEKT id]* refused or turned away

relaxed *[rih LAKSD]* calm; at ease

remedial *[rih MEE dee ul]* correcting

reminded *[rih MYND uhd]* thought of something again

remote *[rih MOHT]* faraway; unsettled

resolved *[rih ZOLVD]* determined; fixed in purpose

responds *[rih SPONDZ]* answers; replies

resulted *[rih ZULT uhd]* happened because of something

romance *[roh MANS]* a feeling of love and adventure; affection

rotation *[roh TAY shun]* taking turns in a regular order; one following the other

S

scenery *[SEE nuh ree]* painted pictures or hangings for a stage

scholar *[SKOL ur]* a professor; a person of learning

sense *[SENTZ]* a feeling or impression

shelters *[SHEL tuhrz]* places that give cover or protection

singular *[SING gyoo lur]* worthy of notice; remarkable

skill *[SKIL]* the ability to use one's knowledge in doing something

somersaults *[SUM ur sawlts]* acrobatic stunts; full body turns, forward or backward

spectacle *[SPEK tuh kul]* an unusual sight; an elaborate show or display

stunt *[STUNT]* a daring trick; a display of skill

substances *[SUB stan ses]* materials from which something is made

success *[suhk SES]* the achievement of something desired

support *[suh POHRT]* to provide for

T

talents *[TAL unts]* special or natural abilities; skills

tenor *[TEN ur]* male singer, often in opera

terrain *[tuh RAYN]* the ground

text *[TEKST]* words and sentences together; a story

translated *[trans LAYT id]* put into words of a different language

trapeze *[tra PEEZ]* a short horizontal bar, hung by two ropes, on which aerialists perform

trophy *[TROH fee]* a prize, often a silver cup

tuck *[TUK]* to pull in; to draw in closely

U

undergo *[un der GOH]* to experience; to go through

upset *[up SET]* distressed; disturbed

V

venturesome *[VEN chur sum]* seeking adventure; daring; bold

visibility *[viz uh BIL uh tee]* ability to see

W

weary *[WEER ee]* tired; worn out

widows *[WID ohz]* women whose husbands have died